GROWING GARDENS

Flower Gardens

BY LIBBY WILSON

Kids Core
An Imprint of Abdo Publishing
abdobooks.com

abdobooks.com

Published by Abdo Publishing, a division of ABDO, PO Box 398166, Minneapolis, Minnesota 55439. Copyright © 2026 by Abdo Consulting Group, Inc. International copyrights reserved in all countries. No part of this book may be reproduced in any form without written permission from the publisher. Kids Core™ is a trademark and logo of Abdo Publishing.

Printed in the United States of America, North Mankato, Minnesota.
052025
092025

THIS BOOK CONTAINS
RECYCLED MATERIALS

Cover Photo: Shutterstock Images
Interior Photos: Tatevosian Yana/Shutterstock Images, 4–5; Jesse Franks/Shutterstock Images, 7; Shutterstock Images, 8, 16 (left), 16 (right), 21, 22, 24, 29 (top); Andriy Blokhin/Shutterstock Images, 10–11; Alex Manders/Shutterstock Images, 12; Eli_Asenova/E+/Getty Images, 15; Yakobchuk Viacheslav/Shutterstock Images, 18–19; iStockphoto, 25; Irina Wilhauk/Shutterstock Images, 26; Sacit Bulut/500px/Getty Images, 27; Quang Ho/Shutterstock Images, 28 (top); Jan Phanomphrai/Shutterstock Images, 28 (bottom); Dontrell Mompoint/Shutterstock Images, 29 (bottom)

Editor: Christa Kelly
Series Designer: Katharine Hale

Library of Congress Control Number: 2024948981

Publisher's Cataloging-in-Publication Data

Names: Wilson, Libby, author.
Title: Flower gardens / by Libby Wilson
Description: Minneapolis, Minnesota: Abdo Publishing, 2026 | Series: Growing gardens | Includes online resources and index.
Identifiers: ISBN 9781098297381 (lib. bdg.) | ISBN 9798384919902 (ebook)
Subjects: LCSH: Gardens--Juvenile literature. | Gardening--Juvenile literature. | Flowers--Juvenile literature. | Horticulture--Juvenile literature.
Classification: DDC 635.9--dc23

CONTENTS

Growing flowers can help people learn about nature.

CHAPTER 1

A Pretty Patch of Flowers

Chris bounced down the porch steps early one morning. She stopped to admire her flower garden. Pink petunias sparkled with dew. Bright purple phlox swayed in the breeze. But the towering magenta ironweed in the back stole the show.

A butterfly landed on one of the ironweed's flowers. Chris had made sure to grow plenty of native flowers. They provided food for the area's butterflies and birds.

Chris got rainwater from a barrel under the shed roof. She soaked the soil around each plant. Then she pulled up the weeds poking through the **mulch**. Last, Chris snipped dead

Native Flowers

Native plants are plants that have grown in an area for thousands of years. They were not introduced by humans. Native flowers provide food and habitats for wildlife. They are often easier to care for than non-native flowers. Most need little watering or **fertilizing**.

flowers from the phlox. She smiled. Working in

the garden always made her happy.

Growing Flowers

People plant flowers for many reasons. Many

like the pretty blossoms. Working with nature

is also good for people's mental health. And

growing flowers benefits the world. The plants

provide shelter and food for insects and

other animals.

There are more than 400,000 kinds of flowers. People use them to create unique gardens. Desert gardens bloom with flowers that need almost no water at all. Fairy gardens are filled with tiny flowers. Pollinator gardens provide food for insects and birds. Each garden is brimming with beauty and provides a fun way to connect with nature.

Christine Capra teaches people to use gardening to improve their mental and physical health. She says:

> Flowers lower stress levels and anxiety in people. . . . whether it's in your outdoor garden or in your home or going to visit a **botanic** garden.

Source: Sandy Cohen. "Embrace the Mental Health Benefits of Flowers." *Shondaland*, 19 June 2023, shondaland.com. Accessed 1 Nov. 2024.

Comparing Texts

Does the quote support the information in this chapter? Or does it give a different perspective? Explain how in a few sentences.

Window boxes are great options for people without yards or porches.

CHAPTER 2

Planning a Flower Garden

The first step in planning a flower garden is to choose a spot for the plants. Some people plant flowers in their yards. Others plant flowers in containers on porches. Still others grow flowers in window boxes.

Gardeners should make sure their garden spot will get enough sunlight. Many flowers grow best with at least six hours of direct sunlight each day. Gardeners growing plants in the ground should also make sure they have good soil. Garden soil should have lots of **nutrients**. Soil can be improved over time by adding **compost**.

Choosing Flowers

Once gardeners have selected a spot for their plants, they can choose which flowers to grow. Gardeners should choose flowers that will grow well in their area. Different flowers grow best in different **climates**.

Garden Maps

Some people make garden maps to help plan their gardens. These maps show where different plants will go in a garden. Making garden maps can help people picture what their gardens will look like.

Hardiness zone maps can help gardeners determine what plants will grow well in a given region. These maps divide countries into zones according to each area's lowest temperatures. Gardeners can check which zone they are in. Then they can choose plants that grow well in that zone.

Annuals and Perennials

Most gardeners plant both annuals and perennials. Annuals are plants that bloom all season. But they live just one year. They must be replanted each spring. Perennials live for three years or more. They bloom for only a short time each year. They go **dormant** in the fall and regrow in the spring.

Pansies are popular annual flowers.

Annuals and Perennials

Annuals

- **Complete their life cycles in one year**
- **Bloom the entire growing season**
- **Grow quickly**

Perennials

- **Live for three or more years**
- **Bloom for part of the growing season**
- **May not make flowers during their first year**

Some people prefer growing only annuals or only perennials. Others grow a mix.

Perennials bloom at different times. Some bloom in spring, such as violets and creeping phlox. Others such as bee balm and coreopsis bloom in the summer. Flowers such as asters and black-eyed Susans bloom in fall. Gardeners can plant perennials that bloom at different times. This will give their gardens color at different times of the year.

Loosening garden soil helps
plants get water and air.

CHAPTER 3

Growing Flowers

Once the garden is planned, the planting can begin! Gardeners must first prepare the garden space. They should remove large rocks and weeds in the planting area. Then they can use a shovel to loosen the soil. This gives the plants' roots space to grow.

Some gardeners add fertilizer to the soil. This adds nutrients to the dirt. The nutrients help plants grow.

Planting Flowers

Some people plant seeds. Other people plant flowers that are already blooming. Seeds are cheaper. But they can take a long time to grow. Gardeners can choose which they want to plant. Both can be purchased at gardening stores.

Gardeners can plant their flowers outside after the last frost. People planting seeds should follow the instructions on the seed packet. These packets often tell gardeners how far apart seeds should be planted. The packet also says how deep to plant the seeds.

People planting sprouted plants, or seedlings, should dig a hole the size of the pot. Gardeners can then carefully remove the plant from the pot and place it in the center of the hole. They can then refill the hole.

Caring for Flowers

Flower gardens need care to stay healthy. One of the most important ways gardeners can help their flowers thrive is by regularly watering their plants. The amount of water a garden needs changes depending on weather, plant size, and plant type.

People can see if plants need water by checking the soil. Gardeners can poke a finger into the soil. If the soil is damp, the plant does not need water. If it's dry, the flowers need water. Gardeners should water the base of the plant. This sends the water straight to the roots.

Fertilizer

Many gardeners fertilize their flowers. Some use organic fertilizers. Organic fertilizers are made of natural plant materials. Other people use synthetic fertilizers. These fertilizers use human-made chemicals. Using too much synthetic fertilizer can damage the soil. The chemicals also hurt animals.

Gardeners should also weed their gardens regularly. Weeds steal nutrients and water from plants. This slows the growth of garden plants. Tall weeds can also block sunlight from reaching flowers. Gardeners should weed their gardens at least once a week. This keeps weeds from making seeds. Then there will be fewer weeds to pull later.

Some plants need to be trimmed. This is called pruning. Gardeners should prune

dead stems. They should also cut off dead flowers. This is called deadheading. This stops plants from forming seeds. Instead, they make more flowers.

In the fall, flowers will lose their color and die. Some perennials can be left in the garden.

Birds can eat the seeds. But other flowers should be trimmed. Gardeners can cut the plants a few inches above the soil. This will help the plant grow back healthier in the spring.

Gardeners should research the best way to care for each plant. Once spring arrives, gardeners can start again.

Further Evidence

Look at the webpage below. Does it give any new evidence to support Chapter Three?

Planting a Wild Garden

abdocorelibrary.com/flower-gardens

Garden Plants

Black-eyed Susan

Black-eyed Susans are native to parts of the United States and Canada. Each flower has yellow petals surrounding a brown seed head. They bloom from June to October.

Petunia

Petunias are native to South America. They come in a wide variety of colors. They bloom from spring until fall.

Purple coneflower

Purple coneflowers are native to parts of the United States and Canada. Each flower has pink petals surrounding a red-brown seed head. They bloom from July to October.

Tulip

Tulips are native to Turkey. They come in many different colors, including red, orange, and yellow. They bloom in the spring.

Glossary

botanic
relating to plants

climates
areas with specific weather patterns

compost
natural materials that have broken down and can be used to help plants grow

dormant
in plants, a state in which plants stop growing, usually during winter

fertilizing
using fertilizer, a substance that is added to soil to help plants grow

mulch
a protective layer of material that is spread on soil

nutrients
substances that living things need to grow and stay healthy

Online Resources

To learn more about growing flower gardens, visit our free resource websites below.

Visit **abdocorelibrary.com** or scan this QR code for free Common Core resources for teachers and students, including vetted activities, multimedia, and booklinks, for deeper subject comprehension.

Visit **abdobooklinks.com** or scan this QR code for free additional online weblinks for further learning. These links are routinely monitored and updated to provide the most current information available.

Learn More

Bell, Samantha S. *Pollinator Gardens.* Abdo, 2026.

Farley, Christin. *The Little Book of Flowers.* Bushel & Peck, 2023.

Gosling, Livi. *My First Garden.* DK, 2023.

Index

About the Author

Libby Wilson's favorite annual flowers are bubblegum-pink landscape petunias. She grows perennial cardinal flowers, coreopsis, and ironweed. In the spring, her woods are covered in marsh marigolds, trillium, and Dutchman's breeches. When she's not gardening, Wilson enjoys researching and writing books for young people about history, nature, and inspirational people.